LONDON'S NORTH
Circular W

The **Northern Heigh**
miles long, taking in
Hampstead and Ham

Its **350 points of interest** – one every sixty yards - consist in equal number of historic buildings, associations with famous people, places or natural or scientific interest and illustrations of Britain's social history.

The circuit is divided into **five sections**. Each section starts and ends at a point easily reached by **public transport** and served by **pubs and cafés**. Though each section makes a good walk in its own right, sections can be **easily combined** to create a more challenging itinerary.

After a few days on the crowded tourist trail of central London the Circuit provides a refreshing opportunity to re-connect with **nature** and to explore those aspects of Britain's **heritage** which can't be found in the centre of so large a city.

The route and its documentation have been devised by **The Highgate Society** with the assistance of the Heath & Hampstead Society and the City of London's Hampstead Heath team.

The unique charm of Hampstead and Highgate Villages is that their streetscapes still mostly contain buildings from the 18th and early 19th centuries when they were **rural settlements**.

On Hampstead Heath, which connects them, **common grazing land** and **farmland** has miraculously survived relatively little changed since Medieval times. Its fringes offer superb examples of landscape architecture whilst its views over London have inspired some of England's most celebrated poets and painters.

The five richly illustrated guides to the Circuit all come **with detailed route maps**, instructions on how to follow the trail and a brief description of each point of interest.

A companion trail to the Northern Heights Circuit, the 15 mile long **Hampstead Heritage Trail**, takes in a further 500 points of interest along its 15 mile route linking **Camden Town** and **Alexandra Palace** via Hampstead and its Garden Suburb.

SECTION 4
South End Green to Golders Hill Park

**South End Green • Hampstead Ponds • Jack Straw's Castle
West Heath • Golders Hill Park**

Planning your trip

The walk starts at the 24 bus terminus at **South End Green** and ends at the café in **Golders Hill Park**. Allow a minimum of two hours for the 2.2 mile walk.

The first section of the walk duplicates the end of section three of the Northern Heights Circuit. If you have already walked that section you may prefer to walk up East Heath Road and re-join to walk at point of interest 36.

Almost the entire walk is across Hampstead Heath and can be quite muddy in places. Stout shoes are recommended.

This section of the Northern Heights Circuit will be enjoyed by people who like a vigorous walk in the open air. It is spectacular in late October when the leaves turn. In winter months make sure to set out in the middle of the day when the risk of getting lost is less. Children who enjoy an active walk will find plenty to interest them.

For a longer walk you could continue beyond Golders Hill Park using section five of the Northern Heights Circuit. You could walk as far as Kenwood House which, like Golders Hill Park, lies a stone's throw from the 210 bus route linking Archway and Golders Green Underground stations.

It would be equally enjoyable to walk this section in the opposite direction.

Facilities

At the start of the walk in South End Green there are many cafés and restaurants (**Le Pain Quotidien, Starbucks, Hampstead Tea Rooms, Dominique**) and a pub with a beer garden (**The Garden Gate**). Other than the **Freemasons' Arms** there are no further refreshment points until you reach the café at **Golders Hill Park** at the end of the section.

There are public toilets at South End Green, on Hampstead Heath midway along the walk, at the zoo in Golders Hill Park and at Golders Hill Park Café.

Daunt Books in East Heath Road contains a selection of books on Hampstead and the Heath.

Reaching South End Green

South End Green is the terminus of the 24 bus route. The 24 runs every 7 minutes from **Pimlico** via Victoria mainline station, Trafalgar Square, Tottenham Court Road, Warren Street and **Camden Town** Underground station (20 minutes). It can also be reached using the C11 bus from stop "E" outside **Archway** Underground station and by the 168 bus from Waterloo via Camden Town and Holborn.

Journey time from Oxford Circus should be about 35 minutes.

Returning from South End Green

Return from **Golders Hill Park** using bus 210 or 268, destinations **Brent Cross** or **Golders Green**, to **Golders Green** Underground station, three minutes, two stops. Golders Green Underground station is on the **Edgware** branch of the Northern Line. Alternatively take the 268 to Hampstead (Northern Line), Swiss Cottage (Jubilee) or Finchley Road (Jubilee and Metropolitan).

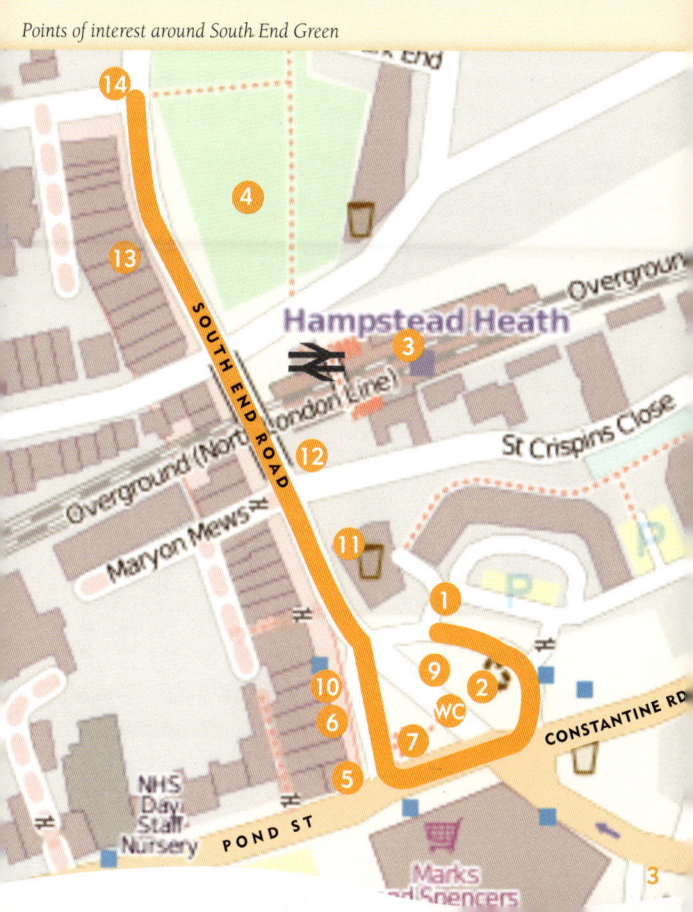

Points of interest around South End Green

The Walk

South End Green pond, 1828

1. This section starts at the terminus of the 24 bus route at **South End Green**. The spacious bus stand was designed as a turning point at the end of a horse drawn **tram route** which reached South End Green in 1887.

2. The **public toilets** beside the terminus were opened in 1897 for the benefit of passengers. They are worthy of a visit if only in their capacity as a listed building.

3. First settled in the 16th century, South End Green was a peaceful hamlet until the arrival of the railway. The **Hampstead Heath Overground** station lies on the route from Stratford to Richmond and Clapham Junction. Revived since being taken over by Transport for London, it will soon form part of London's first **orbital** suburban railway.

4. When it was opened in 1867 it brought large numbers of East Enders to South End Green from where they would enjoy **donkey rides** on Hampstead Heath.

Representation of Hampstead Heath in "Punch", 1860

5. Walk across to "Le Pain Quotidien" on the corner of Pond Street and South End Road. It replaced a bookshop at which **George**

Orwell (1903-1950) once worked. He lodged next door with the proprietor.

George Orwell worked where Le Quotidien now stands

6. Whereas section one explained the number of pubs in Highgate by reference to the requirements of travelling drovers, the number of eateries along South End Road reflects the size of the crowds that used to visit Hampstead Heath on **public holidays**.

Today it is difficult to imagine that the settlement was one of the first mass **tourist destinations**, fulfilling a similar function for East Enders as Blackpool later did for Northernersand Brighton for South Londoners.

Hampstead Tea Rooms

Fountain, South End Green

7. Such was the level of alcohol consumption among these visitors that in 1889 a local benefactor, **Anne Crump**, presented the community with the drinking fountain on the green to the right "to help stop intemperance and vice".

Homilies from notable former Hampstead residents are inscribed in the stonework around the fountain.

8. Meanwhile in 1876 the maltreatment of donkeys that gave rides to tourists contributed to the formation of a Hampstead branch of the **Royal Society for the Protection of Cruelty to Animals**.

9. Just as Pond Square in Highgate bears testimony to a now filled-in village pond, so South End Green's Pond Street, which leads from the terminus of the No 168 bus up past the Royal Free Hospital towards Haverstock Hill, commemorates the **pond** that used to stand where the No 24 buses now park.

⑩ By contrast the 168 route ends directly on the street. Local residents and traders have made vigorous representations to Transport for London, so far unsuccessfully, to have its terminus **relocated**.

Contentious terminus of route 168

⑪ Continue along the left side of **South End Road** towards Hampstead Heath Overground station.

The exterior of the mock-Tudor "The Garden Gate", with its pleasant beer garden, now looks dated and tired. Look more closely above the entrance door and you see interesting early examples of the use of **Arts and Crafts** decorative elements such as exposed beams, stained glass, tile creasing and herringbone brickwork.

Early Arts and Crafts decorative details above the "Garden Gate"

⑫ During the 1960's a major threat to South End Green was a proposal to build a relief road around central London using a mix of viaducts and tunnels. The route planned for this "**Motorway Box**" would have resulted in a motorway viaduct close to Hampstead Heath Overground station, similar in character to Westway, the only section of the route which was eventually built.

The **South End Green Association** was formed to fight these proposals which were discarded once the era of cheap oil came to an end. A notice board on the railway bridge details the association's activities.

⑬ Further along the road **Daunt Books** stocks local guides. Beyond the bookshop turn left into **Keats Grove**, until 1910 known as John Street.

Points of interest: Downshire Hill and Keats Grove

14 Note the finger point sign on the corner, carefully formed by cementing **ceramic tiles** into the brick wall.

Victorian street name and finger sign

15 The initials "S P P M" on the original but relocated cast iron bollards immediately on the left hand side of the road refer to St Pancras Parish Middlesex. These, the road sign and the gas lamps combine to demonstrate the importance the Victorians attached to the design of what we now refer to as "**street furniture**".

16 Nevertheless No 12a, the **modernist** house immediately on your right, does not look out of place in this, the most historic of streets.

17 Quite apart from its association with Keats, Downshire Hill and Keats Grove are virtually unrivalled in terms of literary and artistic associations. The poet and critic **Edith Sitwell** (1887-1964) lived in Keats Grove, as did the playwright **Alan Ayckbourn** (born 1939) at No 11a and **Sarah**, daughter of Coleridge, who would have crossed the Heath from Highgate to visit her. The Liberal Prime Minister **Herbert Asquith** (1852-1931) lived at No 12.

Modernist house, Keats Grove

18 Shortly on your left is the house, previously known as **Wentworth Place**, which was the home of the romantic poet **John Keats** between 1818 and 1820. The building is now a **museum** dedicated to his life and to poetry in general. Opening hours are from 13.00 to 17.00, Tuesday to Sunday (March to October) and Friday to Sunday (November to February). Listed as grade I, the main building is maintained by the City of London.

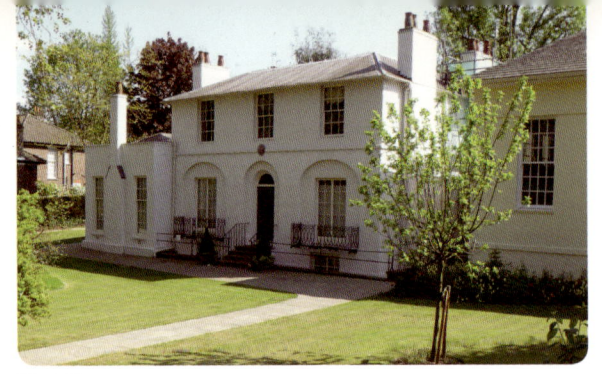

Keats House

The **Romantic** movement, on which Keats was a major influence, reacted against the 18th century Enlightenment's reliance on scientific enquiry and rational thought. Romantic writers such as Keats re-asserted the importance of emotion, passion and exposure to the natural world.

19 A renewed interest in the aesthetics and ethos of the Medieval period resulted in the emergence of a **Gothic Revival** architectural style which dominated London architecture from the early 19th century until the arrival of modernism in the 1930's.

20 Wentworth Place dates from 1814. In 1920 it was threatened with **demolition** to make way for a block of flats. A campaign to purchase it for use as a memorial museum was successful, thanks to many generous donations from the United States. It was opened to the public in 1925.

Entrance to Keats Library

21 The building immediately beyond Keats House is the **Keats Community Library**, a public library which in 2012 was threatened with closure. Note the inscription on the iron entry arch.

Victorian street light, Keats Grove

22 Keats Grove is one of a number of streets in Camden where special efforts have been made to maintain or restore its original **Victorian street lights**.

Quality streetscape, Keats Grove

23 Note too the efforts the Council has made to maintain the high quality of the **foot pavement**, with its slabs of York stone and granite kerbstones.

24 In conservation areas such as this reducing the thickness of **yellow lines** also serves to enhance the environment.

St John's, Downshire Hill

25 At the top of Keats Grove, at the junction with Downshire Hill, stands the distinctive grade I listed church of **St John's, Downshire Hill**. Most churches built to serve London's burgeoning suburban congregations were built in a style that mimicked that of a Medieval church. St Anne's, which you may have passed during section three, is an example, as is St Michael's Highgate, whose spire you see from Kite Hill.

By contrast St John's was designed in the classical style typical of 17th and 18th century churches built in central London. With its wooden weather boarding and its bell tower it would not look out of place in New England.

26 St John's is also unusual in that it does not administer to a local parish. Ordinarily the Church of England would finance new churches to serve recently arrived residents in newly created suburban parishes. By contrast St John's was funded by **private subscription** and it continues to operate outside the normal administrative structures of the Church of England.

The wooden **box pews** which line the sides of the church are those for which the first congregation and successive generations paid pew rents until the early 1950's. St John's is one of the few churches in England retaining original examples of this form of seating.

The church was extensively restored in 2004.

27 At the junction with Downshire Hill turn sharply to the right. **Downshire Hill** has many artistic associations. The painter **John Constable** lived for a while at Nos 25/26. No 21 bears a plaque to the art expert Sir **Roland Penrose** (1900-1984), biographer of Picasso and a leader of the Artists Refugee Committee which assisted refugees from Germany in the 1930's and whose headquarters were at No 47. The first minister of St John's Church, the classical scholar **William Harness**, was a close friend of the poet Byron.

A plaque at No 25 commemorates the Nobel Prize physicist Sir Peter Medawar.

28 Downshire Hill was developed in 1817. In contrast to the regularity of Georgian house fronts, the stucco (ie white plastered) **Regency villas** that line the road are each built to a unique design, notwithstanding the pleasing harmony of the whole. Features of particular interest on many of the houses are the patterns of the iron grilles behind the glazing above the front doors.

Regency architecture, Downshire Hill

Decorative door designs in Downshire Hill

Such are the vagaries of taste that these houses were relatively poorly regarded in the 19th century and Downshire Hill only recovered its status as a **prime residential area** in the 1930s.

29 The more recent infill building, No 13 Downshire Hill, is popularly known as the **Bunny Hutch**. It was designed in 1936 by Michael and Charlotte Bunney, and not named after Bunny Austin (Wimbledon finalist, 1932 and 1938), although he lived at No 7! Michael Bunney was one the architects of the Hampstead Garden Suburb Trust.

30 The **Freemasons' Arms**, a gastro-pub at the foot of Downshire Hill, is notable for having London's last skittles alley in its basement and formerly a Pell Mell court in its garden.

31 Just beyond the Freemasons' Arms turn left into **Willow Road**. You could be forgiven for overlooking the modernist block of three houses immediately on your left, **1-3 Willow Road**. They were designed by the Hungarian communist émigré architect **Ernö Goldfinger** (1902–1987), who lived with his family at No 2. Prior to that they lived at Highpoint in Highgate (see section one).

The Freemasons' Arms

Goldfinger was strongly influenced by **Le Corbusier** under whom he studied in Paris. He and his English wife moved to London in 1934. Throughout his work Goldfinger applied consistently the modern movement principles to which he had adhered since his student days.

From the 1970's Goldfinger's designs became increasingly discredited, mainly because of their association in the mind of the public with the practice of housing social tenants in **tower blocks**.

Superior standards of construction, however, compared with many rival projects, helped to protect Goldfinger's reputation within the architectural profession and what is perhaps his most iconic building, **Trellick Tower**, a 31-storey brutalist block of council flats in North Kensington, is now a grade II* listed building.

32 One local resident offended by the demolition of the cottages which 1-3 Willow Road replaced was **Ian Fleming** who reacted by naming the James Bond adversary and villain "Auric Goldfinger". Goldfinger considered litigation.

1-3 Willow Road

2 Willow Road has been acquired for the nation by the **National Trust** and is its first "modernist" property. Inside visitors can see the Goldfingers' collection of modern art, including work by **Henry Moore**, some personal possessions and characteristic modern furniture during guided tours.

33 Across the road from 1-3 Willow Road is a children's **adventure playground**. Return back down Willow Road to Downshire Hill, turn left and cross East Heath Road, the busy road separating you from Hampstead Heath.

34 At this point you will see a small green hut, now a ranger's office for the City of London which administers the Heath. Here there were chaotic scenes on summer holidays in Victorian times as up to a hundred owners of unlicensed donkeys competed for visitors' custom. There is a 19th century **cattle drinking trough** a hundred yards up East Heath Road.

35 At the junction of Downshire Hill and East Heath Road is one of a number of new tastefully designed "**finger posts**", erected by the City of London to help visitors better find their way around.

New style finger posts, East Heath Road

36 When you have crossed East Heath Road make your way along the contour of the hill where you will reach the lower end of the lowest of three expanses of water. The **Hampstead Ponds** were dug in 1700 by **The Hampstead Water Company**, an early instance of the "private sector" investing in a "infrastructure" project, in this case the supply of water to London's growing population.

37 A founding director of the company was **William Paterson** (1658-1719), who also founded the Bank of England. The ponds replaced a malarial swamp.

(38) The ponds form part of the course of one of two arms of the **River Fleet**, a tributary which joins the Thames at Blackfriars. The Fleet gives its name both to Fleet Street, for many years the home of Britain's newspaper publishers and a collective term for Britain's press, and Fleet Road, the main road south from South End Green.

The name "Fleet" aptly describes the fast flowing character of this river which drops over 400 feet in just five miles. Its fast flow keeps its water clean and clear which has made it an **attractive source of water** for supplying the needs of the City of London.

(39) At the bottom end of the lowest pond, the first you reach, children may enjoy a good view of the water fowl from a gated and fenced **viewing platform** which overlooks the pond.

Coots, mallard and black-headed gulls at the bird viewing enclosure

(40) The villas of **South Hill Park** on the opposite side of the ponds enjoy magnificent views over the Heath as well as the ponds. This has led to the installation of picture windows, sun lounges and attic studios as though the houses looked out to sea.

Owners of these late 19th century homes enjoy magnificent views across Hampstead Ponds

41 Today a major source of conflict arises as householders attempt to further enlarge their homes with **basements**, a practice that is particularly disruptive for their neighbours. Because of the heavy London clay on which many of these houses stand, basements often have a particularly adverse structural affect on other properties not least because they disturb existing drainage patterns.

Their impact often extends to houses and trees on the water courses flowing under the Heath and the neighbouring streets.

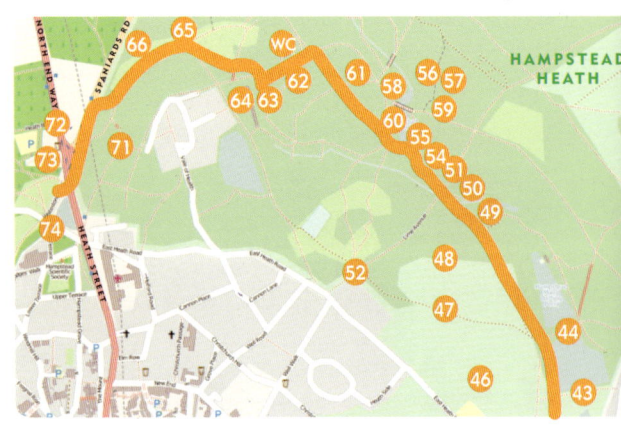

Points of interest, Hampstead Heath section

42 Another source of contention is the practice of commercial **dog walking**, an activity that some would like to see licensed.

43 Continue along the path beside the ponds. They form a series, similar in character to the Highgate Ponds which you may have passed during section three of the walk and which are fed by the other branch of the **River Fleet**.

44 Just before the second causeway that you reach, the one which is between the mixed bathing pond to the left and the No 2

Commercial dog walking near Hampstead Ponds

pond to the right, strike off leftwards from the main path and follow a **sandy dirt pathway** up the hill keeping the bushes to your right.

(45) The view to the left is dominated by the bulk of the **Royal Free Hospital**. Founded in 1828, it re-located to its present site in 1978. Employing 7,000 staff, it is one of London's leading teaching hospitals.

(46) To your left is the site of a **fairground**, set out in 1865, which was just one of the entertainments that attracted 19th century day trippers to the Heath. It still operates on summer bank holiday weekends.

(47) The path you are on is one of many well worn tracks which crisscross what has traditionally been used as **common land**.

Such land provided a vital resource in Medieval times for grazing animals, for "gathering winter fuel" (as in the Christmas carol) and for cutting turf. Such commons were particularly frequent in areas with sandy, acidic soil which were unsuitable for arable farming. The absence of trees and bushes to your left illustrates the impact on the environment of **heavy trampling** by human beings.

(48) On your left patches of bright green grass and yellow iris indicate the location of **boggy springs** caused by the juxtaposition of the sandy Bagshot Beds and the impermeable London Clay.

(49) The winding path continues along a steeper sloping section of short grass on thin sandy soil. The irregularities of such landscapes are common in the rural scenes depicted by both classical and romantic painters.

(50) To your right the thickets of bushes and low trees along the valley bottom provide an important habitat for birds and insects. When this part of the Heath was purchased

Yellow Iris

for the nation in 1889, it was expressly stated that its natural state should be retained. This was one of the first instances of public open space being maintained as a "**wilderness**" area rather than as a formal park, as was the case in the 18th century and in the manner of the Kenwood Estate which features in sections five and one.

51 At the valley bottom the path meets an unmetalled roadway between an avenue of lime trees. This was built by London County Council as a route linking Hampstead and Highgate. The campaign to prevent this route being used by motorised traffic was another victory for the preservation groups which predated the **Heath & Hampstead Society**, currently the leading civic community group on this side of the Heath.

52 This roadway enters Hampstead at **Well Walk**. In the 18th century the iron salts in the waters of its wells enhanced Hampstead's reputation as a **therapeutic** centre, much as its celebrated psychotherapists do today.

53 Hampstead's water was so much cleaner and softer than that of the City of London's that the village thrived as a centre for **starching** and **laundering** the clothes of London's residents. The **gorse bushes** which covered the sandier parts of the heath were then used for airing and drying.

Area of botanical interest below Lime Avenue

54 Crossing this roadway, known as Lime Avenue, bear slightly to your right, taking care now to keep the valley on your left. Its clay river bottoms, sandy ridges and combination of north and south facing slopes, made the Heath an attractive location for many early **botanists**. The Society of Apothecaries visited the Heath regularly in the early 17th century in search of botanical specimens.

55 The track quickly rises to a surprising prospect – a brick **viaduct** crossing a small ravine beyond a lake.

56 Behind the viaduct you may be lucky enough to see a **water rail**.

The Viaduct

57 The part of the Heath you have now entered is **East Heath**, the eastern section of the original **Hampstead Heath** – which has been extended over the years by the public purchase of the Kenwood Estate and the farmlands of Parliament Hill Fields.

58 During the middle and second half of the 19th century a bitter dispute arose over the entitlement of **Sir Thomas Maryon Wilson**, the owner of this common land, to realise the potential **development value** of the land, both for minerals and speculative building.

The **track** across the ravine was laid out in the mid 1840's by Sir Thomas Wilson in preparation for this development. It continues downhill across the causeway between the Hampstead Ponds, ending on East Heath Road by the old fairground.

59 The area to your right provided copious supplies of **sand** for the mortar used in laying the bricks of what is now the Eurostar terminus at **St Pancras Station**. Thickets on the right contain land that was at one time leased out for the manufacture of yellow stock bricks using deposits of London clay. Sir Thomas's roadway thus became an important supply route for building materials.

Brickfields by the viaduct, c 1880

60 Continue to the left up the steep slope. The lack of vegetation is due to the **rabbits** that thrive in the sandy conditions. Then continue up hill along Sir Thomas's roadway up the hill through stands of mature woods.

61 Just off the main path are two **Wild Service** trees. These rare trees seldom grow other than where there was once ancient woodland. Their fruit was at one time used as a remedy for colic and to flavour beer.

Fruit and foliage of the wild service tree

62 After seeing the Wild Service trees, continue quite a bit further until you comes to a path going in two directions. Bear to your left and you will soon see on your right an **imitation Tudor building** which houses public toilets for both men and women.

Built in 1889 they are listed grade II. They originally served as offices for the **plant nursery** serving Sir Thomas Maryon Wilson's projected East Park.

63 Beyond the public toilets taking a left fork you will see a round building with a conical roof dating from the 1840's. Some believe this was a **gate keeper's lodge**, others an "**ice house**". Ice houses were quite common before the advent of electric refrigeration and were situated near ponds and often in woods at some distance from housing. A brick-lined pit below a domed roof would be filled with layers of straw and ice.

The ice house or gate-keeper's lodge

64 Beyond and below the hut is a well preserved example of a "**ha-ha**", an earth ditch fronted on one side by a brick retaining wall. Ha-has were a common feature of 18th and 19th century landscape design. Their purpose was to prevent grazing animals encroaching on the ornamental gardens and lawns surrounding a house. A sunken ditch was considered a less visually intrusive means of achieving this than the erection of a fence.

The ha-ha

(65) Shortly afterwards the path opens up into a flatter area of grass. During the Napoleonic wars this was used as a parade ground for the **Loyal Hampstead Association**.

(66) As the pathway opens out you reach an area used each spring as the site of a travelling **fairground**. To the left is an avenue of pine trees through which you can enjoy a most attractive view across the City.

View across London from above the Vale of Health

(67) Below you is one of a number of very ancient hamlets which developed across the Heath, the **Vale of Health**. Formerly known as Hatch's Bottom, it was renamed when a swampy piece of land was drained and turned into a small lake in 1777.

The Vale of Health from its pond

68 The Vale of Health was a favoured destination for the romantic poets of the early 19th century. This was due both to the wild and natural environment that encircled it and to it being the home between 1816 and 1821 of **Leigh Hunt** (1784-1859), an influential figure in the Romantic movement and friend of Byron, Shelley and Keats. **D H Lawrence** also lived here for a while.

69 When the railway reached South End Green the peaceful nature of the Vale of Health was disturbed by **tea rooms** that exploited its newfound attraction as a destination for donkey rides.

70 This is the only place in London where, after a hundred years' absence, you can now see the **tube-web spider** (Atypus affinis). The spider thrives on grassland where rabbits graze.

71 Visible from this part of the walk is a **pound**, a listed building dating from 1787, in which stray or unauthorised animals were held until recovery.

72 The path in due course reaches a summit close to **Heath House**, the highest house in inner London. It was for many years owned by the Quaker anti-slavery campaigner **Samuel Hoare**. He and his descendants were members of a bank that still trades under Hoare's name.

73 The weather-boarded **Jack Straw's Castle** is reached via a pedestrian crossing. There was no "Jack Straw", this being a generic name used to describe a farm worker. Despite its appearance the current building dates only from 1962. It was formerly a pub; an inn has stood on this spot since the 16th century. The space around the pub was licensed for bowling in the 17th century. **Charles Dickens** is said to have read manuscripts in the inn.

A light-hearted re-invention of 18th century style, its creator was **Raymond Erith** (1904-1973). His chief claim to distinction is his restoration of 10 and 11 Downing Street during Harold Macmillan's premiership.

Jack Straw's Castle

74 To your left is **Whitestone Pond**, at 440 feet the highest point in inner London. This pond was an important landmark on the road between Hampstead and **St Albans** and until recently had extensive views westwards as well as south-eastwards over London.

Whitestone Pond at the turn of the 20th century

In 2010, following proposals put forward by the Heath & Hampstead Society, the pond and its surrounds were restored to its original shape by Camden Council and English Heritage using granite and York stone. The filtration system and reed bed keep the water clean and prevent the growth of algae.

75 Many old photographs show horses using the pond to drink or to cool themselves and perhaps for the wheels of wagons to be cleaned. The ramp allowed the pond to be used by the horses of the **Kings Troop** which until 2012 regularly rode here from their base in St John's Wood.

Whitestone Pond, 2010

76 Whitestone Pond is thought to derive its name from the white **milestone** situated just beyond the pond at the entrance to Hampstead Grove.

77 Close by is a tree planted to commemorate the 50th anniversary of the **United Nations**.

78 You might wonder why major coaching routes should climb the two highest points in inner London, Whitestone Pond and Highgate Village, rather than detour round them. By keeping to **watersheds** these routes reduced the need to cross streams and boggy ravines. Equally important in the days before highway engineering, the risk of carriages **toppling over** was less on routes that avoided running along the sides of hills.

79 As late as the 17th century the crossing of this section of the Heath could be made hazardous by **highway robbers**. Close to the current flagstaff bodies of robbers were hung on a gibbet to deter others.

80 In the 16th century, when views were less impeded by trees and houses, the site was an important link in a network of **beacons** used for giving advance warning of enemy attack, for example by the **Spanish Armada**. The beacon was located where the flagstaff now stands.

81 The distant views and good visibility attracted the painter **John Constable** who lived in a cottage close to Whitestone Pond in 1819. Constable used this part of the Heath as a setting for many of his most memorable paintings, notably westwards to **Harrow on the Hill**. Its exposure to wild weather and openness to the clouds appealed particularly to the Romantic sensibility.

Hampstead Heath, looking towards Harrow 1821, John Constable

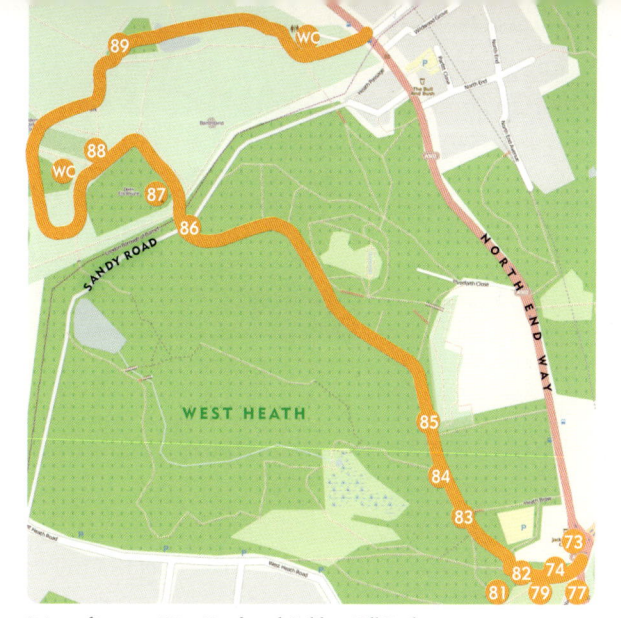

Points of interest, West Heath and Golders Hill Park

82 From the flagstaff, keeping Jack Straw's Castle on your right, take a small path between dense overgrowth down a short incline and then bear right into **West Heath**.

83 Continue along this path through mature mixed woodland which is particularly colourful in autumn. Brambles and mossy hollows below provide a habitat for rabbits and foxes. **Silver birch** and **holly** are particularly common due to the acidic soil, much of which is poorly drained.

84 Look or listen out here for one of the three **woodpecker** species found on the Heath.

85 In due course you will see, rising on your right, what initially appear to be the ramparts of a fortification, with visitors strolling along its walls. This is the largest and most elaborate example of a **pergola**, a horizontal trellis supported on posts that carries climbing plants and may be used as a covered walk.

West Heath

23

Pergolas were popular in the late 19th century as a place to stroll amid rambling **climbing plants** and the scent of roses. Work on this particular one was commenced in 1906.

The pergola from below

Section five includes the walk along the top of the pergola and explains the reason for its construction by **Lord Leverhulme**, owner of Inverforth House nearby.

86. Winding gradually downwards along this path in due course you reach gates through which you enter **Golders Hill Park**. Formerly the grounds of an 18th century country estate owned by Queen Victoria's surgeon, it was purchased on his death in 1898 and is now maintained by the City of London. From this entrance you will enjoy distant views to the west and north-west of London, across **Golders Green**, **Hendon** and **Mill Hill**.

From here on dogs should be kept on leads.

87. To your left is an enclosure containing **fallow deer**.

88. Walking round this enclosure to the left brings you to a recently renovated **children's zoo** and aviary, to public toilets and to an **adventure playground** in a pleasant setting.

Deer in Golders Hill Park

89. From the zoo walk back along the contour of the hillside, crossing an **ornamental stream** via a hump backed bridge until you come to a **water garden** and formal **flower gardens**. Continue up the hill until you come to the Golders Hill Park Café and its terrace.

Ring tailed lemur in Golders Hill zoo

90 The café is situated on the site of the former **Golders Hill House**, destroyed by a bomb in 1941. The flower gardens are situated in what used to be its kitchen garden.

The water garden at Golders Hill Park

91 After refreshments you may want to continue along section five of the North London Circuit, via the pergola, as far as **Kenwood House**. To do this take the path immediately in front of the café terrace. It takes you up the hill to a gate between a line of trees.

Golders Hill Park

To return from the café to Central London by public transport, walk up the path from the entrance to the café until, in fifty yards, you reach the entrance gates on **North End Way**.

On the left is a stop from which you can take a 210 bus (destination **Brent Cross**) or a 268 bus (destination **Golders Green Station**) to the entrance to Golders Hill Underground station on the **Edgware** branch of the Northern Line, three minutes, two stops.

Alternatively, from the stop across the road you can take a 210 bus (destination **Finsbury Park**) every eight minutes as far as **Archway** Underground station, on the **High Barnet** branch of the Northern Line, 23 minutes, 14 stops. This stop is also used by the 268 bus (destination **Finchley Road**) which runs every 12 minutes to **Hampstead** Underground station, on the **Edgware** branch of the Northern Line, six minutes, three stops and thence to Swiss Cottage (Jubilee Line) and Finchley Road (Jubilee and Metropolitan Lines).

Further information

At www.northernheights.eu you can order the other booklets in this series, join the Society and provide feedback.

More detailed information about Hampstead and Highgate can be found in:

Denford, Stephen, The Hampstead Book
– The A-Z of its History and People, 2009

Farmer, Alan, Hampstead Heath, 1984

McDowall, David, and Wolton, Deborah,
The Walkers Guide to Hampstead Heath, 2006

Wade, Christopher, Hampstead Past, 2002

© 2012 Highgate Society

Series Editor: Richard Webber

Publisher: Northern Heights Publications,
10a South Grove, London, N6 6BS

Distributor: www.northernheights.eu

Designer: Nicholas Moll Design

Printer: Rainbow Print Wales

A CIP catalogue record for this book is available from the British Library.

ISBN: 978-0-9572079-4-3

The information was correct as of May 2012. We ask for your understanding where changes have occurred since that date.

All rights reserved. No part of this publication may be reproduced, stored in a retrieval system, or transmitted in any form or by any means, electronic, mechanical, photocopying, recording or otherwise, without prior permission from the copyright owners.

Except where specifically acknowledged or where we have been unable to trace copyright, copyright of the photographs belongs to Northern Heights Publications. These can be reproduced under the provisions of the commons creative licence arrangement.

While every effort has been made by the author and the publisher to ensure that the information contained in this guide is accurate and up to date as at the date of publication, they accept no responsibility or liability in contract, tort, negligence, breach of statutory duty or otherwise for any inconvenience, loss, damage, costs or expenses of any nature whatsoever incurred or suffered by anyone as a result of any advice or information contained in this guide (except to the extent that such liability may not be excluded or limited as a matter of law).

The Highgate Society

The Highgate Society was founded in 1966 to organise resistance to proposals to turn Highgate High Street into a lorry route. Today it has 1,400 members.

Thanks to the dedication and professional expertise of its members, the Society has gained an enviable reputation over the last 50 years for making Highgate a better place in which to live and work. Highgate is one of London's finest conservation areas and the Society protects its unique character by:

- Lobbying central and local government on matters of planning policy

- Working with residents, developers and planning departments to ensure high standards of development

- Campaigning for better public transport

- Playing an active role on consultative groups advising on the management of local open spaces

The Society sponsors a range of social and community activities, including an annual summer fair, winter carols and programmes of summer walks and winter talks.

The Society reports its activities through its quarterly magazine Buzz and regular e-mail bulletins. Its headquarters in Pond Square is open for coffee every Saturday morning from 10.30 to 12 and provides an informal planning surgery.

New members are welcomed and those with special interests and skills are encouraged to participate in the work of our Environment Committee and in our social activities. For more information, contact The Society at 10a South Grove, Highgate N6 6BS, or see **www.highgatesociety.com**

North End Road
NORTH END ROAD
King Alfred School
Park Avenue
Park Drive
The Park
DJ's Jungle Adventure Soft Play
West Heath Avenue
Wellgarth Road
Hampstead Way
Wildwood Road
North End
North End Avenue
A502
Inverforth Close
Sandy Road
West Heath
Heath Brow
NORTH END WAY
HEATH STREET
West Heath Road
Lower Terrace
Upper Terrace
Hampstead Scientific Society
Judges' Walk
Branch Hill
Redington Road
Templewood Avenue
Templewood Gardens
Heysham Lane
Spedan Close
Redington Gardens
Oak Hill Way
Oak Hill Park
Oakhill Avenue
Windmill Hill
Frognal Rise
Frognal
Hampstead Grove
The Mount
Holly Walk
Holly Hill
Hampstead Parochial School
Frognal Gardens
Church Row
Frognal Way
Perrin's Walk
Chesterford Gardens
Greenaway Gardens
Bracknell Way
Bracknell Gardens
Heath Drive
Ferncroft Avenue
Hollycroft Avenue
Rosecroft Avenue
Croft Way
Kidderpore Gardens
Elm Walk
Beechworth Close
Frognal Lane
Finchley Road
A41
Cannon Hill
West End Lane
Langland Gardens
Lindfield Gardens
Ellerdale Road
Arkwright Road
London Borough of Barnet
London Borough of Camden